Miriam Bretones

The Art of Table Decoration

The Art of Table Decoration

by Jane Cornell
Introduction by Letitia Baldrige

THE WARNER LIFESTYLE LIBRARY

WARNER BOOKS

A Warner Communications Company

THE WARNER LIFESTYLE LIBRARY

 Created by Media Projects Incorporated

Copyright © 1980 by Media Projects Incorporated
All rights reserved.
No part of this book may be reprinted without written permission
   from the publisher.

Photography by Ed Rager
Illustrations by Creston Ely
Flower Arrangements by Zibby Tozer, The Flower Service, N.Y., N.Y.

Staff, Media Projects Incorporated
Carter Smith: President
Beverly Kempton: Senior Editor
Bryan Dew: Designer
Ellen Coffey: Editorial Assistant

Contributing Editor: Jane Randolph Cary

Photographs:

Title Page: Courtesy of Horchow Mail Order, Inc.
Page 68: Courtesy of Neiman Marcus By Post gift catalogue
Page 93: Feliciano
Page 18: Roy Thigpen

Warner Books, Inc., 75 Rockefeller Plaza, New York, N.Y. 10019

 A Warner Communications Company

Printed in the United States of America
First Printing: October 1980
10 9 8 7 6 5 4 3 2 1

Library of Congress Cataloging in Publication Data

Cornell, Jane.
    The art of table decoration.

    Includes index.
    1. Table setting and decoration. I. Title.
TX879.C67   641'.8   80-14447
ISBN 0-446-51213-3 (hardcover)
ISBN 0-446-97475-7 (U.S. pbk.)
ISBN 0-446-97770-5 (Canadian pbk.)

Also in The Warner Lifestyle Library
The Art of Gift Wrapping

Contents

Introduction		6
Chapter 1	Elements of the Table	8
Chapter 2	Coordinating the Elements	18
Chapter 3	Centerpieces	30
Chapter 4	Settings with Style	44
Chapter 5	Types of Tablesettings	68
Chapter 6	Special Occasion Settings	78
Acknowledgements		94
Index		95

Introduction

One of my favorite songs of all time is an old Fred Astaire-Ginger Rogers classic. Remember "The Way You Look Tonight"?

The creative host wants his or her guests to react to the look of the table with the same feeling — what a lovely way to look tonight.

Any party is an object lesson in creativity. It's like a patchwork quilt of different segments, each linked to the other, each of equal importance, each an integral part of the whole. Putting the guest list together is the first act of consideration — deciding who will best mix with whom, who relates to whom, who counterbalances who.

Selecting the food is another important exercise in creativity. Food is not only a factor that adds to a guest's enjoyment of an occasion, it is also a basic component of the design of a party.

Let us not forget *the look of the table.* It is another equal factor in the design success of any party. Whether you are setting a buffet for ten on a sun-warmed patio, an after-theatre supper for fifty by the roaring fire, a cozy lunch for four on a card table, a pretty tea table for the meeting of the benefit committee, or a hunt breakfast for thirty in the country — the ambience and theme of the occasion is cast by the way in which the table is set.

It is all very simple. The attention you give to the look of your table tells *how much you care about your guests.*

You can simply plunk down the elegant family silver candelabra, add a florist's arrangement in the center, and then finish the table with your finest linens, silver and crystal. The result: *elegant blah.* Anyone of means can do that, just by opening the cupboards and moving objects from one place to another.

Or you can be creative — a creativity that has nothing to do with lavish decor, the spending of big bucks, the hiring of butlers, and the presence of crystal chandeliers overhead. The creative table depends instead on a thing called *personal taste* and *flair*. It's an extension of the host's personality—and his or her "caring." If there is a "green thumb" in gardening, there is a "deft hand" in table setting. It means combining everyday, even trite elements in inventive ways, so that everything looks new and fresh. It means utilizing "surprise" in the overall design. It means when someone presents you with a bunch of beautiful flowers, instead of grouping them in the traditional bowl, you put one blossom at each guest's place—in a tiny vase, water-filled cigarette urn or perfume flacon. It means covering your table with burlap, serving food in seashells, and placing pieces of driftwood down the center. It means fashioning a gay Maypole with ribbons tied from the overhead lighting fixture to a small favor at each guest's place. It means cutting squares from cheap and colorful fabric remnants to make plain white tablecloths look rich with the designed squares thrown over them. It means taking Aunt Minnie's wedding present out of the closet—a Victorian monstrosity of a sweetmeat tree—and making it sensational with its little crystal baskets filled with fresh parsley and daisies.

This book will help start your creative juices flowing, because your own ideas are the most important. By reading what others do, by training your eye to appreciate and to analyze well-conceived original design, what you do with your table will assume a new excitement.

This book will be a stimulating one for you to read. Enjoy its attractive pictures; then let your imagination flow. *Be yourself* in the decoration of your table. Use what you have around your home in new combinations. Put your personal stamp on your table each time guests appear. Then watch how they will sing to themselves, as they approach the table, "Oh but you're lovely—just the way you look tonight."

Letitia Baldrige

Letitia Baldrige

Elements of the Table

Fork left. Knife right. Spoon just right of the knife. Plate in the middle. That is your basic table setting. And that has not changed. What *has* changed is the approach to table decorating. Once, it had to be rigidly formal to be thought proper. Today propriety is making room for personality.

Luckily, there is much now from which to choose—a host of colors, patterns, and textures for table coverings, place mats, and napkins. Candles in all shapes and sizes. Silk flowers and straw ones, and of course, real ones. China, ironware, stoneware, plastic, pottery. Crystal, glass, and plastic again.

It is very gratifying to put together something special that is all your own, and it does not require an extensive inventory. Stripes do not have to mix with prints, but they might. Everything need not match, but it can.

If the basic elements do not match, they should certainly relate closely to one another. Although you will probably begin with a set of basics in one particular style, traditional, say, you can always add another set of basics, perhaps modern, if you so choose.

Whatever your fundamental set is, the variety you bring to it will depend largely on accents. You can extend the use of your dinnerware and create very diverse looks by covering your table one time with a cloth and the next with straw mats.

In the setting opposite an elegance is evoked by skirting the round table in blue moire, adding white place mats and napkins, and simple blue candles. Using the same blue-bordered plates, fine sterling, and cut crystal, though, you could convey a totally different feeling by covering the table with a cloth of a tiny, sprightly blue print on white.

Choosing Dinnerware
(Plates, Cups, and Saucers)

When choosing dishes, look first for what appeals to you. Does your eye always turn to stoneware, or porcelain? Also, you will probably be looking at price, which has a way of making certain choices more or less attractive.

Once you have settled the esthetics think about your choice in terms of its serviceability and whether it will stand up under the wear you intend to give it. Here are some helpful insights:

China, porcelain, and bone china are all fine china, a category esteemed for its resistance to chipping and its translucent and flawless surfaces—hence its beauty.

Stoneware is opaque, very durable, usually thick and soft-edged. It has a slight grayish tint.

Ironstone is much like stoneware—heavy and durable—except that it is typically white.

Pottery is thick, prone to chip easily, and porous.

Ovenware is subjected to a firing process that renders it heat-and cold-resistant. Durable and fine-grained, today it is in all major lines of fine dinnerware.

Buy the basic elements first—dinner plate, cup and saucer, or mug—and add small plates and bowls later.

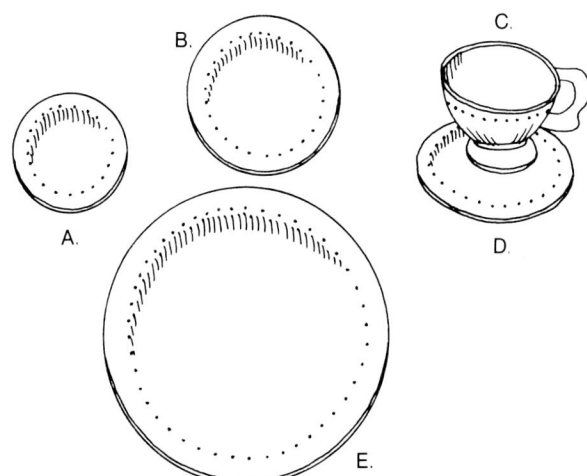

A. Bread-and-butter plate
B. Salad or dessert plate
C. Teacup
D. Saucer
E. Dinner or luncheon plate

A. Tumbler
B. Water goblet
C. Wine goblet
D. Champagne

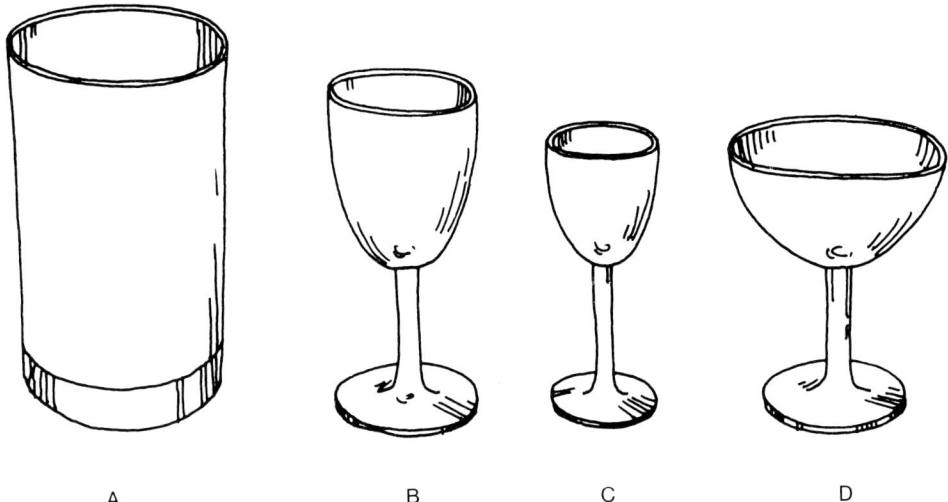

Choosing Glassware

The terms glassware and stemware denote containers for beverages other than hot tea or coffee. Crystal is therefore included in this category.

The range of glassware and stemware is extensive. You will find all the opulence or classic simplicity you could possibly want. When making your selection, consider your style preferences, the kinds of glasses you need, how often and in what settings they will be used, how much money you want to spend, how much storage space you have. As with dinnerware, buy only what you need.

Glasses for water and cold drinks are used most often. Expensive ones may be a joy to own, but the less costly are just as serviceable, and are available in many interesting designs. If you are working within a budget you might want to save here and splurge on stemware for wine. As glassware and stemware stand vertically, look for those with bases weighty enough to reduce the hazard of tip-overs.

Choosing Flatware

Most flatware is made of sterling, silver plate, gold plate (or was until the price of precious metals soared), and stainless steel. While gold plate will probably not be seen for a while, silver may yet weather the storm, though at a cost prohibitive to many. But there is still stainless steel, which is available in traditional silver patterns. And new techniques have made it possible to lighten and brighten the metal to a near-silver sheen. There are other reasons for taking stainless steel flatware seriously — it is strong, durable, and does not tarnish. Some of the latest designs have handles of china, bone, or marble-like plastic, thus making them even more versatile. In short, today's stainless steel can adapt to just about any table.

No law demands that you have more than one set of flatware. If it is chosen wisely — for durability as well as style, period, and pattern — one set will do nicely for everyday as well as for entertaining. Buy the basic knives, forks, and spoons — plenty of extra spoons — and two serving spoons. Add extras, such as salad forks, butter knives, iced-tea spoons, as you wish.

A. Salad Fork
B. Dinner or luncheon fork
C. Dinner or luncheon knife
D. Teaspoon
E. Soup spoon

Added Elements

These are the serving pieces, linens, candle holders, and centerpieces that contribute so much to the total effect of the well-conceived table. More important, they are essential for the gracious presentation of food and drink. Select them as you would accessories for your wardrobe—for variety and versatility. Invest in them the same way, also: Splurge on one or two special pieces, then fill in as your budget allows.

If you are noted for the soups you serve, a splendid tureen will bring cheer to your spirit and grace to your table. If wines are your pride, find a handsome carafe or wine basket—or one of the new terra cotta wine coolers. Should your casseroles rate plaudits, serve them in containers worthy of the contents.

Linens help you stage excitingly different tables with the same cast of characters. Your collection should include place mats and runners, as well as full-scale cloths. And napkins, of course. They can match, complement, or contrast with cloths and mats, and function also as liners for baskets and trays.

Any dinner table or evening buffet looks better by candlelight. Whatever your color scheme, there are candles in colors to match, blend, or contrast. Although the white taper is always correct, candles in the latest shapes and hues add a touch of newness to the table. On the following page is a study in symmetry and flair: ceramic calla lily holders with wine-hued candles.

Centerpiece holders can be just about anything your way of entertaining suggests. Elegant crystal bowls for flowers or fruit, a collection of bud vases for single blossoms, a stately old pitcher for a charming bouquet, a basket for flowering plants or a collection of shells. Start with one or two containers that work well with your china and glassware. These will be reliable standbys until fate or fortune supply you with a cherished one.

**Serving Dishes
Coffee and Tea Sets**

Vegetable dishes, sauceboats, sugar and creamers, coffee and teapots, can be bought one at a time or as part of a complete set along with your dinnerware. A distinguished pattern presented in full array is certainly impressive, but all the components need not match. You may prefer the challenge of mixing patterns and styles. This takes a little time and a careful eye, but is rewarding.

Silver serving dishes harmonize well with traditional china and are always appropriate, if somewhat expensive. However, there are also many styles and patterns in oven-to-tableware that adapt beautifully to traditional settings, as well as to contemporary ones. And now that microwave cookery and one-dish meals are so popular, ovenware is often designed to conform.

Linens

Linens (which are not necessarily made of linen, but often of synthetics) are essentially a basic, but to rank them as such seems a demotion, for these are the mood changers, the scene stealers, and the crowd pleasers. If you are stumped for table decorating ideas, let linens point the way. Have several solid colors—white, as well as pale, vivid, and dark shades. Have stripes and checks, if these fit your dining environment. Do not shy away from the flashy print or the bold geometric. Mix solids with patterns by layering one over the other. Try florals with plaids. Be courageous. Each setting becomes a refreshing new production. Try covering tables with quilts, rugs, bedspreads, or quilted upholstery fabric. Dress fabrics can be converted into mats, runners, table skirts and top cloths. Round out your linen collection with plenty of napkins in colors and patterns to coordinate with cloths and dinnerware. Remember place mats are wondrous time savers: Have them in patterns and solids; in fabric, straw, and vinyl; in wood and metal. Quilted place mats have become such favorites that manufacturers now make channel-quilted tablecloths and skirts in featherweight materials that machine wash and dry.

Vases and Centerpiece Holders

Charm, beauty, a touch of drama—that is what centerpieces are all about. And their holders are no less important than they. Cut crystal, silver, and porcelain vases for flowers; glass, silver, and china bowls for arrangements of flowers or fruit; baskets for arrays of vegetables or breads, or displays of holiday ornaments; pottery or ceramic pitchers and cachepots for flowers or plants. Potted plants, for example, can come from windowsill to table if you have pretty ceramic pots or handsome baskets for them to rest in.

For the sake of your table, be certain all containers for cut flowers and live plants are waterproof. Pottery is porous and will allow water to seep through unless it is glazed inside, or at least has a durable glaze on the outside. Baskets should be lined with a layer or two of aluminum foil, and have a bowl or glass inside if the centerpiece must be kept moist.

Containers should also be sturdy enough to keep arrangements firmly and steadily in place. Tall, soaring compositions need containers that will not tip over easily; so do massive clusters of fresh fruit or heavy-blossomed flowers.

No matter how dramatic a centerpiece might seem on the composing board, if it is too high for seated guests to see over it inhibits across-the-table conversation and is ineffective. Transfer it to a lower container or tray.

Everyone owns at least a favorite vase, but it may not work well on your dinner table. In that case, in addition to cut crystal, silver, and fine china—all versatile choices—be on the lookout for those pottery and ceramic pieces created by talented artists or craftsmen. Not only does their uniqueness add panache to a table, but often they increase steadily in value.

Look, too, for unusual (but pretty) objects that might make interesting centerpiece holders. Shoes—wooden ones—for a bunch of jaunty tulips, old cut-glass toothpick holders for nosegays, are examples. Or tall glass flasks (an idea borrowed from the chemistry lab) for haughty, long-stemmed blossoms—one to a container. Weight the flasks with white pebbles if the high-stepping beauties show signs of tipping.

Candles and Candle Holders

Candles are special; no other light can equal the one they cast. If your room's electric lighting is equipped with a dimmer switch, lower the intensity to just under that of the candlelight. But if the choice is between the lights on or off, turn them off. Remember, however, to add extra candles so your guests can easily see each other and the food.

Candles should be either above or below eye level. Ten-inch candles are suitable with tall holders. Put extra-long ones in low holders. Groups of large round and square candles create interesting and colorful focal points for a table when they are comfortably below eye level.

Keep a supply of graceful white tapers, which are right with everything, but do begin to collect the new shapes and colors: spirals, swirls, and twists; chunky ones, and bulbous ones; animal, vegetable, and flower shapes; in pastel colors, vibrant reds and blues, purples, chocolate brown, or ebony black. These change-of-pace candles are surprise touches you can add to the table in a flash, and all are created to keep abreast of changing trends in interior design. Whether it is Art Deco or French Empire, there will be a candle to reflect the period.

Your store of candle holders need not be extensive, but it should be varied, and include decorative as well as plain ones in china, silver or brass, and glass or wood. With an interesting mix of styles and materials you can adorn a basic china wardrobe in many fashions. Mix heights, also. A group of low, medium, and tall candles is particularly effective. To avoid a discordant look when you cluster candles, put them in holders of a similar material—all brass or all wood, for instance.

Often the candle's base will not fit securely into the holder. If it is too large, trim the excess with a warm, sharp knife. For thin candles, a dab of florist's clay, good in any holder, will keep them firmly in place. Solve the problem of the large, fat candle, which can split or crumble when pressed onto the spike of a holder, by heating the spike before putting the candle on it, or making a hole in the bottom of the candle with a hot nail.

Coordinating the Elements

Creating tables with a total look is an art anyone can master. There are no hard and fast rules, but keep in mind an important principle that makes the difference between an ordinary table setting and one that sparkles. It has to do with accents, the interplay of attractive opposites: dark versus light, rough versus smooth, plain versus fancy. One approach to the total look is to use two basic elements that match, and add an accent. For example, if plates and glassware are the same in color, inject an accent that is different — printed napkins, perhaps. If both plates and flatware have an ornate pattern, accent with simple goblets. Or, if plates and flatware are understated, team them with elaborate glassware.

In most stores that sell table settings and table toppings, you will find the basics already color- or pattern-coordinateed by the manufacturers. Study the displays to learn how well-selected accents can bring a table to life.

Accents are equally important when the three basic elements — plates, flatware, glassware — are of the same period or style: all traditional, or all contemporary. If the basics are lavish, accents should be simple. If the basics are smooth or subdued, accent with strong textures, bright colors, or unusual shapes.

Some of the most original accents to bring to your table are those personal or family treasures you have collected. An example is the heirloom pewter, seen on the opposite page, that adds a mellow quality to the charming family board. The pieces are in perfect accord with the table and the fine old woods of the room's furniture.

When plate and glassware match in color, as they do in the photograph opposite, a printed napkin adds a splash of new color and brings the tabletop alive. It is a simple and economical way to accent any setting. Although, in this case, the basics were precoordinated by the manufacturer, you can color-match new glassware or linens to dinnerware you already own. Take a plate with you when you shop. Sales personnel will understand; they, too, are fashion conscious. Besides, color does not carry well in the head — better to have it in hand.

The fine china and silver flatware shown below, in an ornate pattern precoordinated by the manufacturer, call for simple accents — a glass or goblet plain in line. Add a bright place mat and napkin, keyed to the colors in the china. By the way, the flower is another accent, particularly appealing in its fresh naturalness.

  In the contemporary setting above, all elements have again been precoordinated by the manufacturer, even the flatware. Color, shape, and material are compatible in style and mood. A dark cloth of earthy brown keeps the arrangement in harmony. For lighter notes, a smooth napkin in palest beige and a glass with a hint of warm amber. When a table's color scheme is of closely related hues, as is this one, change the pace. Add a centerpiece of curly blossoms or leaves, for example. Or dried grains and weeds. (More about centerpieces in Chapter 3.) Where contemporary settings feature strong colors or uncommon shapes, go overboard with the intensity of your accents.
  Using contrasts strategically is a challenge, but it is fun, too. Couple stark, solid-color dinnerware with linens printed in broad geometrics or larger-than-life florals. If the boldness is in the dinnerware—and these days patterns can range from cup-sized dots to cartoons—feel free to let a brilliant cloth be the backdrop.

The Big Three

All the basic elements in the fully coordinated and traditional setting shown below are ornate in pattern and styling. Finely etched goblets match the floral pattern of the plates. Enhance their beauty even further by showing off your lace-edged or cutwork linens. Fresh garden flowers or an arrangement of silk flowers in a silver bowl would be perfect on such a table, as would white or pale pastel tapers in silver holders. Votive candles in long-stemmed tulip-shaped glasses would be yet another way to adorn it.

Completing the Picture

When coordinating a table, no detail is too small to consider. The place card holder, for instance. If it fits your particular mode, it lends charm, and can be found in a myriad of styles in silver, gold, cut crystal, and porcelain.

The napkin ring. It too is worthy of high honor as it brings a special note of color and texture to your table setting. Some are exquisitely wrought of shell, bone, ivory, exotic woods, brass, and antique silver.

As you plan and shop for extras, think of the multiple functions each might perform. Costlier pieces ready for double duty can be well worth their price. In a second life, pitchers, bowls, and tall cake plates are centerpiece holders; salad bowls are punch bowls as well as receptables for bread, fruit, flowers, Easter eggs, and Christmas ornaments. Trays are a blessing. As portable tables-in-miniature, their versatility is boundless. They even make sensible, as well as beautiful, foundations for centerpiece arrangements.

Individual ashtrays and cigarette holders are a thoughtful addition to any table, formal or informal. Glass, silver, and brass are the most prevalent materials, but there are also lovely porcelain ones, often made to match dinnerware patterns.

Illustrated on the opposite page are just a few of the more traditional extras. They need not match your dinnerware. Silver, of course, rarely does, nor should it, outside of the museum case. Choose porcelain, ceramic, or pottery serving pieces that complement the material and quality of the basic elements on your table.

Decanters, pepper mills, or marvelous footed bowls are other lively additions. And it is always a good idea to have at least one large platter, for serving pasta, fowl, or a mound of shellfish.

In a moment of leisure, why not draw up a list of those extras you would like to own but do not. When asked what you want as a gift, consult it. Who knows, your wish for a chafing dish, samovar, or hurricane chimney might yet be fulfilled.

Mix and Match

It was inevitable. Someone was bored making look-alike plates, cups, and saucers, and threw in a surprise. Why not a cup from the green batch with a saucer from the yellow one? And the pink plate with a turquoise bowl? Why not mix splashy prints with stripes? Or abstracts with florals? The effect was fresh, new, and exciting.

One of the more lasting rewards of the mix-match happening is the shift in attitude about what goes with what. Unearth your great-aunt's hand-painted dessert plates. They probably are not the eyesore you once thought, and could be spectacular with your silver-banded china. Then go one step further and use silk flowers or linens to echo the delicate tints in the plate. It is a time of resurrection. Plates, cups, and bowls long banished to cupboards can now be taken off the shelf to enhance your table settings.

The art of mix and match is not mysterious. A discerning eye and a modicum of restraint are its only requirements. If you are mixing patterns, keep the colors well coordinated — match color exactly or use just those that blend well. If you are mixing colors, be sure patterns and shapes are in the same style. A plethora of unrelated elements on a table simply looks like its owner got carried away in a secondhand shop.

To mix and match with confidence, take cues from the full table settings in dinnerware boutiques. The designers and manufacturers have almost elevated the concept to an art form. Plates in triple layers, each one different, are an arresting still life of color on pattern on shape. Cups, saucers, goblets, serving pieces, and small accessories are fashioned to interrelate, even though each can be bought separately.

In the early and modest move toward mix-matching, a particular forty-five-piece set of budget-priced dinnerware was widely acclaimed. Its simple shapes and vibrant colors, seen on the opposite page, made it ideal for the casual table. Luckily it is still with us, in variety stores and from some mail-order houses. Pair it with striped or solid linens that highlight one of its colors. Add a bowl of iridescent candles, or boughs of leaves.

Mix and match at its most sumptuous can be seen on the opposite page. Coordinated by a master of the trend, it starts with a fine white china dinner plate widely bordered in black and banded in gold. On top is a smaller plate banded in burgundy and gold and emblazoned with a gold tulip. The black-banded cup and saucer and gold china goblet create further excitement. Notice how the burgundy napkin with its small-scale print strikes a balance with the dense colors and the dramatically oversized tulip motif.

If two work, why not three? The triple layer of plates is another popular direction in table fashion. In the setting above, the first to go on the table is a black-bordered plate, topped by one bordered in a provincial print. And to prove that mix and match can have its moments of frivolity, the third plate boasts a vivid drawing of two hens and a rooster. With double and triple layering, the chance to do the dramatic, the unexpected, the spontaneous, and the beautiful is increased two and threefold. So experiment.

Mix and matching is the proof of a significant change in the way we practice the fine art of table decoration. Once you try it, you are sure to find it irresistible. So, too, will your guests.

Centerpieces

The centerpiece is the table's crown, and unites the elements into a harmonious whole. Once, candles in tall holders and arranged flowers were the norm; they are still the most appropriate at certain times. But the inclination today is to let your inventiveness be your guide. Look to the menu, the color scheme, the occasion, season, or holiday for ideas. Do you have a hobby (or do your guests)? There might be a clue in the answer. Do you collect anything? Clay figures from your travels, baskets, rocks and minerals with their interesting shapes and glowing colors, wood carvings, stained glass, Venetian glass, and shells make intriguing—sometimes amusing—decorations, and create a very personal table. Remember, too, that if anything is an excuse for a party—a friend's new job, perhaps—it can trigger notions for a centerpiece.

No longer need a centerpiece be a single piece, or even in the center. Let it occupy the corner of a small table, enhance one end of a long table, or brighten the back of a buffet. Put arrangements at each place setting or parade flowers or personal treasures down the table.

To determine the correct size for a centerpiece and whether to use a single grouping or a scattered one, set the table and see how much space is left. Keep arrangements low, or tall and slender, so you and your guests can see one another.

One blossom can be dramatic enough to stand alone, as it does on the opposite page; or align several flowers on the table, like a strand of jewels.

Fresh Flower Centerpieces

Unless you have an extensive cutting garden, you will probably buy fresh flowers. Talk to your florist about the kind of flowers available and the mood you wish to convey. You can order by phone, but it is better to shop in person. If the color scheme is paramount, take a plate or napkin with you. If theme is the essence—Oriental, for instance, or Victorian—take one of the key objects you plan to use.

Standard arrangements are available, but most fine florists prefer using their talent to design something special for your occasion. An arrangement can be held in a container from the florist's own collection (its cost will be included in the fee), or you might prefer to use one of your own.

Ask for the latest delivery the florist can manage. If flowers do arrive hours in advance of your party, store them in a cool place (in the refrigerator, if there is room). Bring them to the table after it is set and just before your guests are due.

When budget is a consideration, design the arrangement yourself. A bunch of fresh daisies is always cheerful. Or buy a single perfect blossom, or three (carefully considered numbers are the secret to lively versus listless flower arrangements), and put them in inexpensive slender-necked glass vases.

Keep on hand a supply of glass and plastic liners for baskets and silver centerpiece holders, (plastic containers from the delicatessen are particularly useful); floral tape for anchoring liners to containers; bricks of green, sponge-like Oasis (the material florists most often use in arrangements); frogs (another implement used to hold flowers in a vase); and a quantity of white pebbles or sand for adding weight to holders that need extra stabilizing.

The massed blooms, opposite, richly different in color, shape, and texture, work their magic in this extravaganza held in a splendid silver bowl. With each glance there is something new and captivating. The bulk of an arrangement should be no higher than the distance between one's elbow and wrist—a reliable guide for judging the proper height of a centered table arrangement. Slender stalks give the illusion of height, and can be seen through; they also lend airiness to the overall assembly.

Delicate, amber-shaded, dried grains look especially rich on tables set with earthy pottery or stark white dinnerware.

Forever fresh silk blossoms, seen here in a treasured blue bowl, impart a hint of the exotic.

Silk and Dried Flowers

Silk flowers are back and more sumptuous than ever. Their color, delicacy, and shape are nothing short of fabulous in mirroring the real thing. If you invest in them—and they are costly—spend the extra dollars for the finest: those lavished with the greatest number of petals, the best tints and dyes, the most exquisite detailing. Unlike cut flowers, their glory endures; you will not suffer the trauma of emptying them in the trash in a week's time.

Buy silks singly and arrange them yourself, or ask the store if they will do it for you. Simple compositions of one to three blossoms are generally adequate for table decor. Combine them with an expressive figurine in a shallow bowl, or a single tall twig in a unique shape. Later, you might replace the twig with wand-like blades of slender grass, or such exotic leaves as magnolia, palm, or lemon.

Great multiblossom arrangements are spectacular, but they are expensive, and you can quickly tire of so much massive sameness. Should you invest in one, rely on its plentiful stock to create new compositions. Keep the silk clean and fresh looking by dusting it with a soft toothbrush.

Porcelain and beaded flowers also add beauty and textural interest to centerpieces. Use them as accents in an arrangement of fresh leaves or flowers. Plastic flowers, on the other hand, have become less popular mainly because they are stiff and cold-looking. Unless they are mixed with quantities of real greenery, they detract from the warmth and charm of a table.

Dried flowers, however, are a delightful alternative to short-lived fresh flowers or the pricey silk ones. Dried blooms, delicate grains, even roadside weeds make enchanting table decorations. When allowed to dry on the stalk, plants assume rich earth-colors ranging from the palest beige to dark brown, and often they crack and twist into surprising shapes.

Baskets, crocks, glazed or unglazed pottery are natural choices for holding dried arrangements. So, too, are containers of clear glass, pewter, stark white china, silver, copper, and wood. Florists, and many other shops, stock dried plants. Or harvest your own from the field, shore, or country roadside.

Fun Centerpieces

Do you harbor old toy banks, seashells, miniature railroad cars, oriental carvings, teapots, dollhouse furniture? Original and amusing centerpieces can be concocted with many of your favorite objects. Show off only a few pieces at a time, however. (The display of an entire collection is not the point; the menu is.) Place them directly on the table, on an unframed mirror, or on a tray. Use a footed tray for slight elevation if the pieces are small. To give the arrangement a boundary and highlight its mood, color, and texture, intersperse it with ribbons, bows, blossoms, or banks of fresh green leaves.

Let good taste guide your choice of objects. Anything that shocks is out of place. Beauty and beguilement are the goals. A toy pickup truck loaded with fresh flowers might be a perfect lighthearted touch for an informal gathering of close friends—but it is hardly suitable when the board chairman is first coming to dinner, unless he happens to be in transportation.

Fun centerpieces not only add wit, their elements are usually inexpensive. Indeed, they can often be gathered for nothing. Stash them away for that moment when the mood and setting are just right.

A winter's night and hearty soup might call for a chunky log with crusty bark as a centerpiece. Surround it with leaves, a scattering of pebbles, and ceramic animals. During warmer months, create a miniature seascape with driftwood, shells, and sea birds carved of wood—a squatty old pelican if you happen upon one.

Fun centerpieces for children should contain things they can safely play with at the table and possibly take home. Toys, balloons, or large pieces of a jigsaw puzzle are a few of the hundreds of ideas. (No whistles, though—you will only be sorry.)

The diminutive and purely decorative ceramic houses on the opposite page are exquisite in every detail and immediately suggest any number of compositions. Mimic reality by casting small twigs and flowers as trees and community flower beds. Use ribbon for paths and streets. Plan the idyllic village.

Live Plant Centerpieces

Potted plants are for all seasons. Use them for any occasion in any month of the year. If your timing is right, some will even sprout a bouquet for your table.

Small plants look best when they are grouped on a table. On an intimate table for two, however, put one at each place. Larger potted plants stand alone quite dramatically in both formal and informal settings. Prune any limp or discolored leaves, turn the top soil a little, and clean the foliage with soft cotton and lukewarm water.

Choose plants to fit your table's ambience. If colors are soft and warm, plants should look delicate. If colors are strong, plants should be striking, perhaps spikey, or with big shiny leaves.

If the pot a plant lives in is not right for a festive table, it is of no matter. Simply clean away streaks of soil and dust from the rim and put it in a party disguise: a basket, bowl, urn, mug, casserole, or tureen. Or cover it with fabric: dress material, denim, velveteen, flannel, taffeta, or one of the table napkins you will be using. Be sure to tape a coaster to the bottom of the pot to prevent soil and water seepage from damaging the table. Then set the plant in the middle of a square of fabric, gather the fabric against the rim, and tie yarn or ribbon around it. Another technique uses the talents of double-stick tape to hold the fabric in place. Put the tape around the upper rim of the pot, just to the edge of the pot but not over it. Cut enough fabric to cover the pot, to tuck under the bottom, and to make a fold at the top edge of the fabric and another at the side seam. Fold over the raw top edge of the fabric and the raw edge of the side seam, and press the fabric against the tape around the pot's upper rim. When the top and sides are fitted, gather the bottom fullness into little tucks and secure them underneath the pot with tape that is adhesive on one side only. Tie ribbons in alternating bands of color around the pot, if you wish, or camouflage the seams with perky bows.

The plants on the opposite page, in economical plastic pots covered with a country print cotton, would lend a provincial touch to any table set with pottery or stoneware.

Fresh Fruit and Vegetable Centerpieces

Pumpkin, corn, squash, and other fruits of the harvest have adorned table centers for centuries. Today, when there is no such thing as out-of-season, lush centerpieces can be created year-round with the colors and textures nature so graciously provides: satiny eggplant in deepest purple; peppers in vibrant green and brilliant red; magenta beets; rosy apples; the pale, sweet green of just-ripening pears. Then too, fruits and vegetables provide more variety per pound than most other makings of centerpieces. For sheer opulence, befitting a king, little equals a heaping mound of succulent fruit.

And if you think it must just sit there looking beautiful, think again. Let your guests enjoy it with the cheese course. Even though the fruit is to be eaten during the meal, however, it should not be too ripe. Skins must be firm, full of color, and free of blemishes, while the shapes should be well defined and emphatic. Leave the stems on pears, apples, and cherries for composition. If a leaf is still attached to the twig on a peach or orange, by all means let it be. It adds to the visual appeal.

Fruits and vegetables can be arranged directly on the table, but they look more festive on a tray or in a container that gives the composition form, elevation, and distinction. Fruits should seem to overflow their holder; vegetables, on the other hand, are less flexible, and need more confinement. Baskets, wooden bowls, and large tureens are sturdy enough to keep such arrangements intact.

The dramatic arrangement that needs intricate wiring to hold it together is best left to the artisan chef and caterer. If you have a yen to try it yourself, however, begin with simple forms, and use fruits and vegetables that bruise less easily than others.

On the facing page, turnips (looking for all the world as if they had been painted with a watercolor brush), slender green peppers, and eggplants are nestled in a mushroom basket and tied with a plaid taffeta bow. Below them, a wide, shallow silver bowl holds a composition of fresh fruit. Design a table around such as these. Eat them later.

Candle Centerpieces

Candles, today, are quite spectacular. In a sense, they are bits of sculpture, and as such so decorative that some people collect them the way others collect ceramics. Take advantage of the multitude of shapes and colors, and compose a centerpiece with an impact that belies its relatively low cost. Compared to what you could spend for sensational table art, candles are a bargain.

Make a small grouping of candles in different colors. Be certain, though, to vary their height to avoid the appearance of a battalion of soldiers marching down the table. The candle holders may be unique and beautiful, but they do not establish the boundary such a centerpiece needs for emphasis. To do so, garnish the bases with leaves, real or silk flowers, pebbles, shells—whatever best pinpoints your theme or color scheme. (When candles in their holders are one element among several in a composition they can stand alone, their bases left ungarnished.)

The array of colors and shapes of candles almost boggles the mind. They swoop; they swirl; they soar. Use these exciting forms, rather than the conventional ones, to create centerpieces.

Coordinate candle colors as you do linens, china, and accent pieces. Look for colors that match or blend with the plate or cloth when the mood is to be serene. Go for strong contrasts—red and white, black and yellow—to signal vivacity. A birthday party, for example, might be enlivened with candles in vibrant primary colors.

Textures, as well as shapes, can suggest table themes. Some candles resemble pagodas and are perfect for an Oriental setting. Others feel and look like basket weave; delightful for casual tables. Some glitter and sparkle—champagne for two?

The chunky candles in primary colors on the opposite page would make any table festive, especially circled with fresh galax leaves and accented with real lemons. To lend visual variety, some of the candles are elevated on small blocks of wood.

Settings With Style

Ambience, charm, beauty, distinction, even showmanship. Style is all of these — and more. A dazzling buffet may look like an effortless happening, but it did not get that way by itself. Careful planning and attention to detail play a major part in creating a table setting with style. Uniqueness springs from a basic theme that guides all other elements into place.

Deciding on a theme for your table is a snap when you rely on color for inspiration. Color is a foolproof style-setter. Linens in splashy prints and solids, mixed and matched, give your basic china a wide variety of backdrops. An accent piece in terra cotta, shell, even vivid plastic, can trigger color ideas for the whole table.

Your menu is another starting point. National and ethnic dishes bring china, linens, centerpiece, and color ideas into full play. Decorate a table to complement the kind of food you are serving and compliments will follow.

China, glass, flatware, and linen designs inspired by historic eras form backgrounds for memorable meals. Colonial, French Provincial, Old English, dynasty Oriental, represent just a few of the many modes that can make your table distinctive.

Opulence conveys style, and so does stripped-down minimalism. If ornate table accessories and rich-looking linens bring you joy, go all out and include lavish centerpieces and accents in lush colors. In the opposite vein, stark contemporary dinnerware set around one dramatic focal point creates an understatement that is nothing short of spectacular.

Three distinct moods, for instance, are evoked by three distinctive shapes, opposite page: one in crystal, two in glass.

Traditional English Floral

*"All sorts of flowers the which
on earth do spring
In goodly colours gloriously
array'd."*

—Edmund Spenser

The British love of flowers is reflected in their decorative china. Many of the famous old floral patterns are as popular today as they were hundreds of years ago. Spode, Wedgwood, Doulton, and others are classics now, collected avidly and treasured for their lasting beauty. Modern adaptations have changed little, if at all; most are still being hand-decorated. New patterns are introduced frequently, but stylings hew to the grand tradition—eloquent florals that bestow style and warmth to a table.

Because they are classic, English florals fit into casual and formal settings with equal ease. Accompanying flatware and glasses or goblets may be ornate or simple.

Solid-color linens in pale or dark tones seem, at first glance, to be wise choices for use with English patterns, but do not overlook subtle plaids and stripes. Search for a color in the cloth that echoes one in the plate. Or just set your china on the bare wood, aged and mellow, for a subtly handsome background. Place mats or table runners are as appropriate as a full cloth. A layer of linens—a small circle or square over a floor-length table skirt—gives traditional florals even greater charm.

Fresh or silk flowers and graceful candles in elegant holders are flourish enough for tables with country garden flair. Napkin rings in heavy silver or delicate porcelain work well in formal settings; so too do ties made of ribbon or lace. Heavy cut crystal is a natural complement to English floral patterns, as are goblets and tumblers of silver, pewter, old pressed or blown glass.

If you are a new collector and budget is a consideration, begin with the essentials only: dinner or luncheon plate, cup and saucer, for two or four. Since trends in table design permit greater flexibility, auxilliary plates and soups need not be exact matches, merely complementary in color and material. You can fill out a collection as you go along. Or you may settle for one or two superlative serving pieces to use for food on one occasion, to fill with flowers on another.

An English floral inspired by field and garden flowers, opposite page, with a few classic accessories such as place card holder, napkin ring, hostess bell, tiny urn, demure salt and pepper.

Early American

National pride inspires tableware design in every country. And native pursuits like fishing, hunting, gardening, farming, shipping, are characteristic Early American motifs. Each is definitive enough to spur ideas for tables with style.

Our heritage is also reflected in the colors of Early America. Since pigments came from nature — plants, minerals, tiny river and sea animals — the colors were earthy, subdued rather than sharp: indigo, magenta, ochre, rose madder, umber, saffron. You can invest your table with flavor from an earlier day by starting with linens in rich natural tones. Fabrics with small provincial print designs carry forward the mood, as do soft plaids and stripes, especially if they are handwoven, or look it.

In general, Early American dinnerware is heavy and soft-edged. Characteristic shapes are round and hexagonal, accented with narrow solid-color borders. A center motif is depicted in simple lines. Designs are straightforward, uncluttered, suggesting that accent pieces or the centerpiece be fanciful and high-spirited. Too much plainness can become dull.

Pewter, silver, copper, brass, colored glass, wood, and wicker are appropriate materials to use in Early American settings. Choose objects that blend with the period. Art Deco or ultra-modern free-forms hardly fit. Wrought iron has great possibilities as long as the object is not too Oriental, or too contemporary in design.

Use candles of classic mold, such as spiral, twist, or honeycomb. The early dipped candles had a delightful handmade look that is now copied in mass-produced ones. Select such natural colors as ivory, bayberry, honey, indigo, terra cotta. Scented candles are a matter of personal preference, but remember their odors may conflict with the aromas of a flavorful meal.

The clipper ship was a favorite Early American theme, opposite page, and will be found in browns, blues, maroon: a color cue for linens. A collection of pewter objects strikes just the right note of style.

Funky Forties

Nostalgia has many moods. Who would have thought that as space-age cities are planned we would yearn for the sound of the big band, want to wear harlequin eyeglasses, and eat from green glass plates.

Yes, there is even "retro" dinnerware. From memories spring new realities. This time around, tables can reflect the Forties with fresh spirit and insight. Black and chrome are back. You will see it in stemware, china, linens, in flatware with handles that look like polished slabs of midnight marble.

Vivid, unrestrained colors verging on clash are in. Splashy florals cheek by jowl with bold checks are now considered neat, not gaudy. Dime-store glassware garlanded with improbably large flowers in raw reds, yellows, and blues, so popular in the Forties, is being duplicated by today's manufacturers to add a punch of color to Eighties dining.

If yours is one of many homes with plates, cups, saucers, and bowls from the Forties, use them right along with your current dinnerware as salad or dessert plates, for drinks at the table or bar, for centerpieces—or simply to liven conversation.

Manufacturers like the Forties look, and this time quality of design and material are uppermost in their designing minds. You will find their accomplishments at with-it dinnerware shops and boutiques. If you own Forties pieces, take one with you as you shop for additional place settings or accent pieces to use with your collection. If you intend a full-scale trek down memory lane, entire sets are available.

The Forties flashback trend vibrates with refreshing wit and new ideas. Current translations include all the accoutrements of the table from soup to nuts. By coordinating every element you will indeed create atmosphere. Bold contrasting colors add verve. Even a floral centerpiece could be offbeat—big white lilies, stalks of gladioli, giant silk poppies, flamboyant orchids.

There is Forties bombast in the exuberant present-day setting, opposite page, expressed in sharp black-and-white and vivid red, an unabashed mix of blossoms and flashy checks.

Country Kitchen

The warmth of the rural kitchen represents a way of life so deeply ingrained in our heritage that it has inspired major design trends. Homeowners spend thousands of dollars trying to recapture that mellowness within their modern-day houses. Take heart. You can create the country-kitchen look on your table at far less expense. Admittedly, the homespun effect is not for Regency dining rooms or ultra-sophisticated apartments. But on porches, patios, near sunny bow windows, under the perennial spreading oak tree, country kitchen tables are truly inviting.

Even if you do not possess a thing once owned by Grandmother, stores and shops are filled with instant nostalgia. Quaint prints, gingham, rough-weave fabrics (dress goods all) set style for pennies. Cut the edges with pinking shears to make napkins, or fringe the ends by pulling threads. Or do neither. There are a wealth of ready-made tablecloths, napkins, and place mats dyed in facsimiles of country colors that look slightly aged. Remember the quilted textures, too.

One surefire way to achieve the look is to combine contrasting prints in related colors. Many cloths are made to be reversible for this very reason. Other linens come in mix-and-match collections of cloth, runner, place mat, napkins—maybe a tea cozy.

Neutrals and earth tones, as well as sharp reds, greens and yellows, look inviting on old wood set with ironstone or pottery plates. Flatware has kept pace with trends in kitchen dining; designs in shapes and colors to harmonize with the rustic table abound. While handles and knobs of bone or ivory are classified *endangered species* (or ecologically unethical), today's well-made plastics are more than acceptable on knives, forks, spoons. Furthermore, they are dishwasher safe.

Contrasting prints blend cozily on the country kitchen table, opposite page. Shades of burgundy and rose madder evoke the warmth of a cheery fireplace or nearby stove. Thick, smooth ironstone dinnerware invites a menu for hearty appetites. For accent, tinted candles in squat preserve jars.

Colonial

Tables in the Colonial tradition combine fine china, handsome silver, and delicate crystal on polished wood.

Colonial dinnerware designs are refinements of the lavish English, European and Oriental decorations which characterized an exciting period in world history. Chippendale was beginning to fashion magnificent furniture; new trade routes to the Orient brought rich silks and exquisite porcelains to the West; and Georgian architecture, French Empire, and Directoire became the design symbols of all that was splendid and grand. That was the genesis. From it emerged dinnerware designs with such popular motifs as floral garlands, fruit, the lyre, the Oriental chrysanthemum, the stag, and the pineapple crown.

Colors range from pale pastels to rich shades of red, blue, green, yellow, terra cotta. Thin borders of gold outline plate and cup rims. As a rule, patterns do not dominate the pieces; the proportions are subtly balanced, pleasing to the eye.

Silver, crystal, and glassware are available in faithful reproductions and adaptations of Colonial designs. Colonial table settings were most often on bare wood, though fine damask place mats were also used, and occasionally a table was covered in ivory damask, printed chintz, or burgundy and gold brocade. Dress your table with contemporary fabrics made to resemble many of these glorious materials, confined today primarily to museum collections.

Formal centerpieces of fresh garden flowers in silver or brass bowls, cut glass vases, or Oriental porcelain are in keeping with the Colonial mien. Add white tapers in silver holders and the table will be complete.

Classic Colonial richness is echoed in the table setting of fine china and silver on the opposite page. Sterling flatware and crystal goblets surround a white berry-patterned plate. The white heirloom place mat is edged in openwork embroidery. Individual cigarette urn and ashtray are of silver. A crystal vase holds a bouquet of daisies, creamy roses, and pink carnations.

Oriental

For Westerners yearning for a bit of the exotic, an Oriental menu is an inspiration. Not only is the food quite different, the way in which it is served is also. Every inch of a table can be transformed with fabrics, flowers, dinnerware and eating implements that are unique — but not inscrutable. On the opposite page are but a few of the ingredients.

A footed tray lacquered in deep red for dining on the floor, on a pillow, of course. If you are at the table, use the tray in the center to hold flowers and condiments. The red lacquer napkin holder with its beige napkin, the lacquer chopsticks, and the tall lacquer candleholders go either place. As does the red lacquer fan, which is not simply decorative, but useful. Try it as a tray for small edibles, or as a background for a miniature flower arrangement. The octagonal white china plate, with its fitting dragon motif, rests on an under-plate that is banded in gold and bordered in black. The tall goblet is rimmed in gold, complementing the larger plate. For accent, tiger lily blossoms in a low vase.

Table cloths are not an Oriental custom, but if it strikes your fancy, you might use a runner to resemble a Japanese obi sashaying down the center, or place mats in unusual silk or cotton prints. Choose a fabric (it can be dress fabric) that contrasts or blends with your dinnerware. If your china is white and unadorned, opt for a patterned cloth. (Brightly patterned dinnerware, on the other hand, looks best against plain backgrounds.) Or try tatami — Japanese mats of rice straw bordered in black cotton or wool; they are made for the floor, but give tabletops an interesting texture.

Add a special Oriental touch with a Japanese flower arrangement as a centerpiece. Other decorative touches might be Oriental objects of brass, wood, wicker and straw, clay or pottery, lacquer, and porcelain. Reproductions of ancient animal and mythical figures are especially intriguing.

One final note: chopsticks. Some people handle them well, others do not. Remember those lacking in dexterity but not in manners. They do not want to seem sloppy, so offer forks and spoons.

Oceans and Islands

You can let your imagination take a world tour and come up with table setting ideas from just about everywhere. But certain oceans and islands will always be the most provocative. The Greek Isles, the South Pacific, Cape Cod, the Caribbean. You need not have been there for the mention of them to conjure up images of the charming, the remote, and the romantic.

The brilliant light of a coastal Greek village comes to the small, low table, opposite page, in a dazzle of white, blue, and green. The table, tightly sheathed in blue cotton, sits on fluffy sheepskin. And on the table are set white, blue-bordered china plates rimmed in gold; blue glass goblets; and fat, textured candles. Each polished brass ring holds a sunburst-pleated napkin of vibrant green in its grasp. The table's only deception: its gold coins, in truth merely foil-covered chocolates.

And when you tire of Greece, move on to the South Pacific by covering the table and floor pillows in a vivid blue and floral fabric. Let red and purple stemless blossoms adorn the candle bases, and shell holders encircle deep blue napkins.

For the charm of Cape Cod, leave the table bare. Rope mats—used by boat owners as buffers between ship and dock—become seats. Sea shells and bubbles of glass surround the candles.

Climate can also trigger setting ideas. The Caribbean is hot; its water, azure and turquoise; its sand white; its foliage deep green; and its flora a riot of magenta, yellow and purple. Bring its lush hues to your table with fabrics, candles, and flowers. China, glass and silver play up well to these colors.

If, at heart, you are a wanderer, stay on the move—in spirit, at least. Remember, as you explore, that food is a catalyst. New foods often need to be served in unusual dishes; the color of the food or the pattern of the dish can inspire a color scheme for accents. Then too, the lore and life style of a culture are frequently given expression in small stone, wood, or clay works of art. Use them in a centerpiece to further say where in the world you are.

Victorian

Roses and old lace, elaborate tea tables, and potted palms are remembrances of time past—a time when embellishment was excessive. It was, of course, the Victorian period. Some of the gingerbread may be missing, but Victoriana is back.

China patterns remain dressy and formal, and the colors, lush. A table replete with matching pieces is a stunning sight, especially for purists. But if a mere hint of the Victorian is sufficient, use just a few special pieces to accent plain white china. A Victorian teapot with matching sugar and creamer are always charming. Or teacups and saucers with matching dessert plates.

With Victorian settings, you will want pretty linens, shining silver, and sparkling crystal. Cloths or place mats in pure white or dark solid colors make the best backdrop for richly patterned china, as do table skirts of deep wine-colored velvet or taffeta. Napkins can be frilly or plain, and silver the same, as long as the styling is traditional rather than contemporary.

Fresh flowers belong on Victorian tables: a bouquet of white roses and frothy fern in a silver bowl, mixed blossoms in a vase of cut crystal, or nosegays in little porcelain holders.

Victorian colors are predominantly bold. China patterns come in rich reds, cobalt blues, ripe oranges, hot pinks, and verdant greens; all stimulate ideas for color schemes and accents for your table. Explore shops, attics, old trunks, and auctions for treasures. But do not expect to be alone. The quest for serious Victoriana, early and late, and for tacky Victoriana, early and late, has just begun. Prices are reflecting the vogue, but do not be deterred. The hunt is good sport, and there is always the chance someone will part with a dusty relic that is worth a fortune—or at least several pretty pennies.

On the opposite page is a profusion of Victoriana on a rich brown cloth inset with lace ribbon. The napkin is lace trimmed too, but is in a pale beige to lighten the color-heavy scene. Bone white china is overlaid with big red roses and edged in gold. The ornate silver pattern looks right at home, as do the frisky tiger lilies in amongst the garden flowers.

Scandinavian

In sharp contrast to ornate Victorian dinnerware are the uncomplicated, uncluttered designs of Scandinavia. Their directness appeals to modernists everywhere.

Function and simplicity are the essence of the setting, opposite. The white stoneware mug and soup bowl, decorated with wide brushstrokes of blue, are meant to hold hefty portions of food and drink. Goblets are of thick, clear glass, built low and sleek, and all the easier to hold. The quilted place mat and its matching napkin are in a softly muted plaid; the plain wood napkin ring is smooth, and pure in line. The ridged candles add to the texture and precision.

Some dinnerware seems to spring to life when accompanied by particular materials and colors. This is especially true of Scandinavian designs. Stainless steel, heavy glass (either clear or smoky), teak, and rough-weave wool and cotton fabrics enhance the modern setting. The colors in this dinnerware tend to be either sharp or slightly misty. Let the tones guide your choice of linens and accents.

Dried grains or dried flowers are natural as centerpieces. For fresh flowers choose daisies, chrysanthemums, or field flowers.

Flatware patterns in stainless steel are often plain, almost severe, but nevertheless interesting, as the implements' shapes are usually a variation of what we are used to.

A table set with a Scandinavian flavor brings to mind smorgasbord. If you have not served one recently, or never have, make your next buffet party a smorgasbord. The food is always an adventure—hors d'oeuvres, hot and cold meats, smoked and pickled fish, sausages, cheeses, salads, relishes. Unless your dining room is enormous, let the buffet table dominate it and have small tables for your guests in other rooms. If your dinnerware is white, you might use black or brown cloths or place mats. Choose napkins in an intense color, and have plenty of candles—big, round, textured ones. Skoal.

French Provincial

French Provincial lays claim to the middle ground between Scandinavian and Victorian—at least from a design standpoint. If your moods are mercurial, French Provincial is there to oblige. Neither elaborate nor plain in color, shape or features, French Provincial dinnerware is quite simply all charm.

Small wonder, then, that it is so accomodating. Dress it up, dress it down. The colors can be bright—chrome yellow, sharp blue, definitely pink; or light—pale aqua, rose, teal, blue. Patterns can be stylized representations of stacks of grain, trees, cottages, wildflowers, little plants. As a rule, all the patterns are small. Some appear only in the center of a plate or bowl, while others encircle the rim of a plate, cup, or saucer.

The patterns may be understated, but the forms are not. They are curvaceous, even slightly bulging—but in this case, in just the right places. Plates have shaped edges; handles undulate. Bowls and tureens are large and impressive, and bring high drama to a bare table or sideboard.

For French Provincial ceramics, worn, slightly scarred, old wood is by far a more effective background than a highly polished surface. Rough-textured linens are an appropriate highlight, especially big checked patterns in bonbon colors. If you want a less casual look, use solid color cloths or place mats in deep greens and blues, plum or burgundy. Arrange flowers loosely and informally in pitchers, baskets, or big copper bowls. Studied arrangements are a jarring note in a provincial setting.

For a buffet for four, the antique sideboard, opposite page, is bedecked with French Provincial. Chrome yellow ceramic dinnerware has a pattern of tiny field flowers. The charming covered vegetable dish can double as a small soup tureen or centerpiece holder. Ivory spiral candles in turned-wood holders complement the setting beautifully. For accent, goblets of amber glass, and napkins printed in tones of deep coral and cream.

Stripped Down Modern

Every season sees the birth of yet another design in dinnerware, flatware, and glassware. Some styles depart as quickly as they arrive, others become traditional.

Stripped down modern has a message that is likely to be heard and heeded. Why? Because it says beauty — simple, straightforward, and understandable beauty.

The materials are familiar and comfortable. We have lived with vinyl and stainless steel for enough time to appreciate their potential; no longer are they simply the stuff of unsightly implements. There lies the secret. Today's modern is imaginatively designed and expertly crafted. You will be seeing more of it in stores and shops.

The pieces in the setting opposite are a few of the forecasts of the future that are here to stay. The graceful lines of the goblet blend with and temper the more severe lines of the stainless flatware. And the place mat, while it has an interesting shape and texture, more importantly lends warmth to the setting.

Fabrics have a tale worth telling, also. The channel-quilted table cover is padded with superlight polyester fiberfill, a modern idea that adds softness so easily. For years, to make our tables look inviting, we wrestled with those thick flannel pads under our cloths. At last we have a pad and cover combined in one lovely, lightweight and machine-washable package.

For ambience, give this spare look soft lighting, a background in neutral tones, and a muted free-form centerpiece. In other words, keep accents low-key. The drama of the setting needs no distractions.

Even if you feel a bit safer with the traditional, do not overlook the pleasure of creating a table setting stripped of all pretension.

Types of Table Settings

Unless you happen to have a head of state to dinner, there is no need to fret about finger bowls and service plates. Dining has bid goodbye to the formal. This does not mean that graciousness, beauty, and hospitality have faded away—far from it. With the current emphasis on atmosphere, guests are more pampered than ever. And more relaxed.

In truth, the break with rigid formality is easier on host and guest alike. If fewer knives, forks, plates, and stemware are needed for a splendid meal, does that make the occasion (or the table) less formal? Place mats under the Spode hardly lessen the superiority of your food, or your guests' enjoyment of it. With table decoration raised to the level of an art, dining can be as elegant an experience in the 1980s as it was in the 1880s.

When menu and occasion call for serving three courses, each with wine, more stemware, plates, and flatware, of course, will be used. Even so, you can manage with the three basic elements, augmented with a glass for red wine in addition to the one for white, a salad fork, perhaps, and a soup spoon.

Several small tables for two or four can solve the problem of comfortable seating when your table is not large enough. Plate, knife, fork, spoon, napkin, are the only necessary components of a small setting. A simple low centerpiece, perhaps four candles and a scattering of leaves, as seen on the opposite page, enhances the intimate atmosphere.

Another setting especially suited to today's relaxed but beautiful dining is the buffet. Luncheon and breakfast table arrangements have moved into the spotlight, too, as you will see in the following pages.

Informal and Formal Settings

The informal setting is the one you use everyday. Its main elements, pictured on the opposite page, are customarily sold coordinated in five-piece place settings of dinnerware: three plates in graduated sizes (the salad or dessert plate is not illustrated), one cup and one saucer; and in five-piece place settings of flatware: two spoons, two forks, one knife.

In a formal place setting, there will be stemware rather than tumblers. A goblet for water, for example, plus stemmed glasses for one or two wines. It is traditional, but not compulsory, to place wine glasses to the right of the water goblet. Some hosts feel it is more convenient to have the water goblet nearest the right hand. But if you are moved to reverse the order, do so.

Cups and saucers are not part of a formal place setting, because coffee is served after dinner with dessert. Bread-and-butter plates are optional for formal tables. If you serve rolls, by all means provide plates and individual butter knives.

Even formal settings have relaxed now. When it comes to that dismaying array of utensils — oyster forks, fish forks, fish knives, berry spoons, and so on — only the very basic and necessary pieces need appear. And many of these do double duty. Teaspoons can serve for dessert as well as coffee, while soup spoons can act as small serving spoons for vegetables.

Place card holders, menu stands, napkin rings, individual ashtrays, and holders for cigarettes are most certainly in the formal tradition; however, they are not a necessity, only a matter of personal preference.

Whether your table is formal or informal, it becomes more manageable if you bring a bit of ingenuity and logic to the so-called "proper" format. Successful hosts follow an approved guideline only up to a point, and then add variations of their own. Most often their modifications are determined by their particular style of entertaining, the size of their home, and the amount of tableware they own. Do not be afraid to experiment. Adapt a little, add a little, subtract a little — that's what it is all about. Make the most of your possessions, and your tables will be another expression of your hospitality.

The format for an informal place setting (when no wines are served, and coffee or tea are offered during the meal): *dinnerware*—dinner or luncheon plate, salad or dessert plate (not shown), bread-and-butter plate, cup and saucer; *flatware*—salad fork, luncheon fork, luncheon knife, teaspoon, soup spoon (butter spreader is optional and is sold separately, as a rule); *glassware*—a simple tumbler for water or flavored beverages.

Breakfast and Luncheon Settings

A friend, who is an accomplished artist and expert gardener, gives breakfast parties. She likes the look of the morning sun and the colors of the early day. "Besides," she says, "cut flowers seem fresher, garden vegetables taste better, and when the party is over, I can spend the rest of the day in my studio."

Breakfast is an eye-opening alternative to the evening and late-night celebration, and for many, it is the only time they are free to entertain. Weekend breakfasts are particularly relaxing for those whose careers keep them tied to busy weekday schedules.

A delightful breakfast table setting is the least difficult to achieve. Use your prettiest china, silver, and stemware, and if the morning finds you in a whimsical mood, add gay linens. Layer vivacious cloths over your table, or put dainty place mats on gleaming wood. Add cheery fresh flowers—they brighten even a dreary day.

But should the early hours not be your time, how about lunch? Luncheons are a welcome break in everyone's routine; indeed, even grownups like the notion of playing hooky.

Keep the menu light—soufflé, salad, a simple dessert, coffee or tea. Only the basic dishes and flatware are needed, though you will want a stemmed wine glass if wine is included.

Place mats with matching or contrasting napkins are ideal for luncheon settings. If china and silver are dressy, choose a print or solid color in a pale tone. Casual dishes of stoneware or china look wonderful with textured mats in bold prints or vibrant solids. For extra interest, use place mats with a matching or contrasting color.

Loosely arranged bouquets of flowers and leaves, or a grouping of shells, make lovely centerpieces. For flatware, silver is always a suitable choice, but stainless steel is also more than acceptable.

For breakfast, the simplest setting will do.

A luncheon place setting, with an extra spoon for dessert.

The Circular Buffet

The circular buffet is the technical term for a very popular table-setting plan that adapts as easily to the square or rectangular table as to the circular one. In essence, the table occupies the center of the room, making all of its sides accessible for guests to help themselves to food and drink. There are numerous ways to set a buffet, but logic is the key to the smooth flow of traffic. The diagram on the opposite page will guide you. At the starting point guests should find dinner plates stacked near the main course, usually a generous casserole or chafing dish of meat, fish, or fowl. The serving spoon and fork are placed near the main dish.

Next in line is a vegetable dish with its serving spoon. Around the table and along its left side (going clockwise), a salad bowl and serving spoon and fork. Further along, the relishes. Salt and pepper stand nearby, within easy reach. Then a tray of breads and rolls. (Butter may be individual pats on ice, or the rolls may be already buttered.)

At the far end of the table are the flatware and napkins. Around the table's last side is the coffee service and cups. Guests may serve themselves on the first trip or come back later. Sugar and creamer stand near the cups. In setting the buffet, allow ample space between service dishes for guests to rest their plates. There is nothing so awkward as trying to serve yourself salad with only one hand.

On centerpieces: Whether you have selected fresh flowers for the table or a delectable mound of fresh fruit, make the arrangement large. A skimpy centerpiece on a big table looks feeble.

If the table is of beautifully grained wood, you might want to leave it uncovered. But beware of the potential damage of red wine spilling. And do have thick, heat-resistant mats under the serving pieces to protect the surface and to keep dishes from slipping. If the table is covered, the cloth should be large enough to hang well over its sides and ends. If you do not own one sizeable enough, consider a king-size sheet, crisp and smoothly pressed.

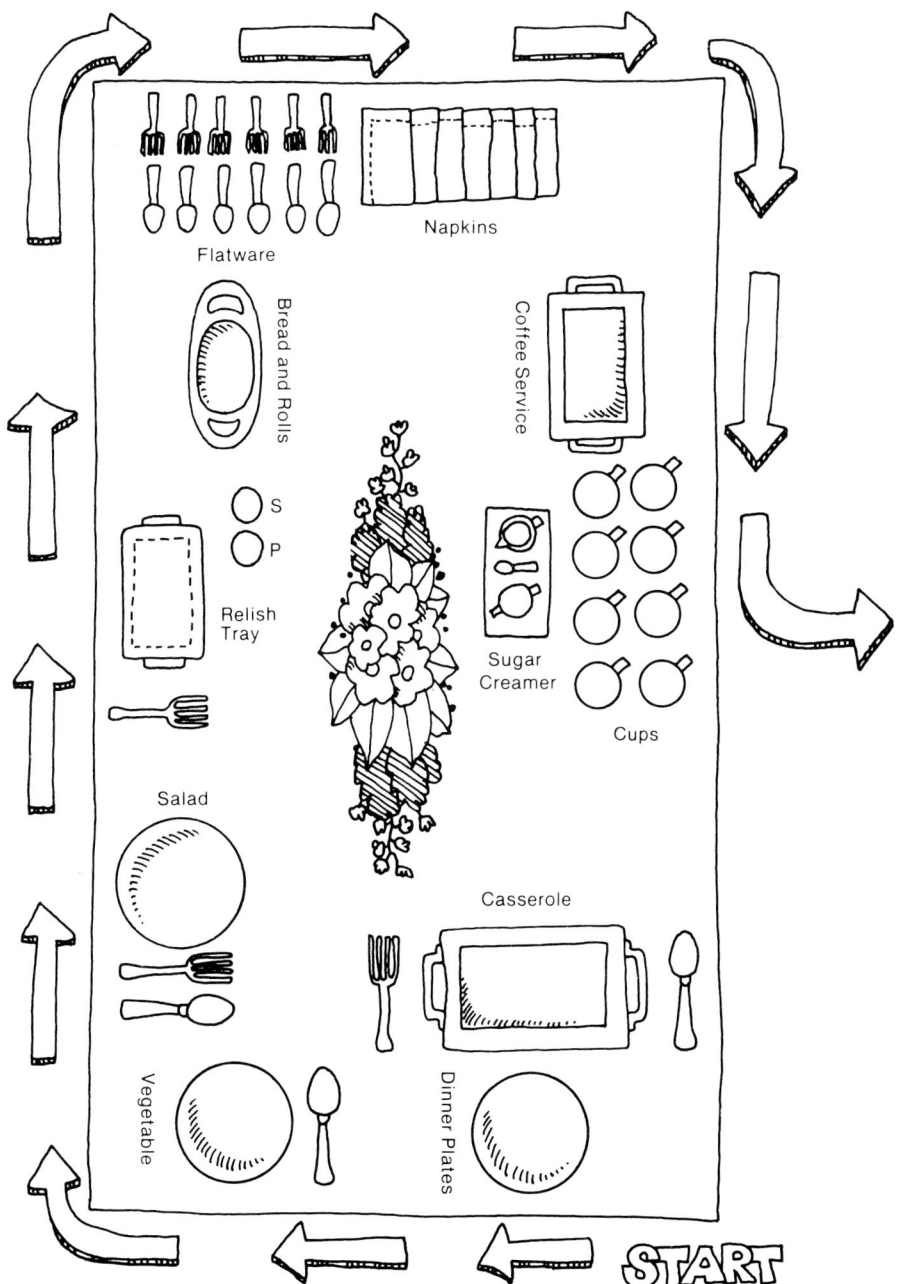

Three-sided Buffet In a room with limited floor space, one side of the buffet table is placed against the wall, and hence unusable, except to hold a centerpiece. If the table is large enough for several serving dishes as well as the coffee service, follow the plan suggested for the circular buffet. If it is not, however, slight alterations may be needed. In the illustration on the opposite page, you will spot the necessary changes. Dinner plates are at the starting point; the main course dish, and its serving spoon and fork, are near the left corner of the table. Along the side, and next in line, is the salad *or* vegetable dish. Breads and rolls are just beyond; salt and pepper, close by. Near the far corner is a relish tray. If you are having a vegetable instead of relishes, the appropriate dish and serving spoon could be placed here.

At the far end are the flatware and napkins. And at a comfortable distance from this end of the table, guests can help themselves to coffee from a tray set on a small table.

Of course, you can modify either of these basic buffet plans to suit your needs. But remember two important principles: Food must be placed within easy reach; and service pieces should be arranged in a logical pattern, so guests need not worry about bumping into one another. It is wise to make a floor plan of the room and the table's position in it. Note where guests will stand while waiting to approach the buffet, how they will move along the table's length, pour coffee, and then leave the buffet for another room. Clear furniture away from doorways so that guests can move smoothly. Even a crowd can be handled without undue chaos if you plan carefully.

With the three-sided buffet, the wall behind the table becomes a perfect backdrop for imaginative staging. Use it to display decorative plates, a beautiful folding screen, posters, a magnificent rug or quilt, macrame hangings — whatever. And because guests need not face one another across the table, centerpieces can be soaring freeform compositions, massive candles in ornate cathedral holders, or outsized bouquets of flowers worthy of a banquet hall.

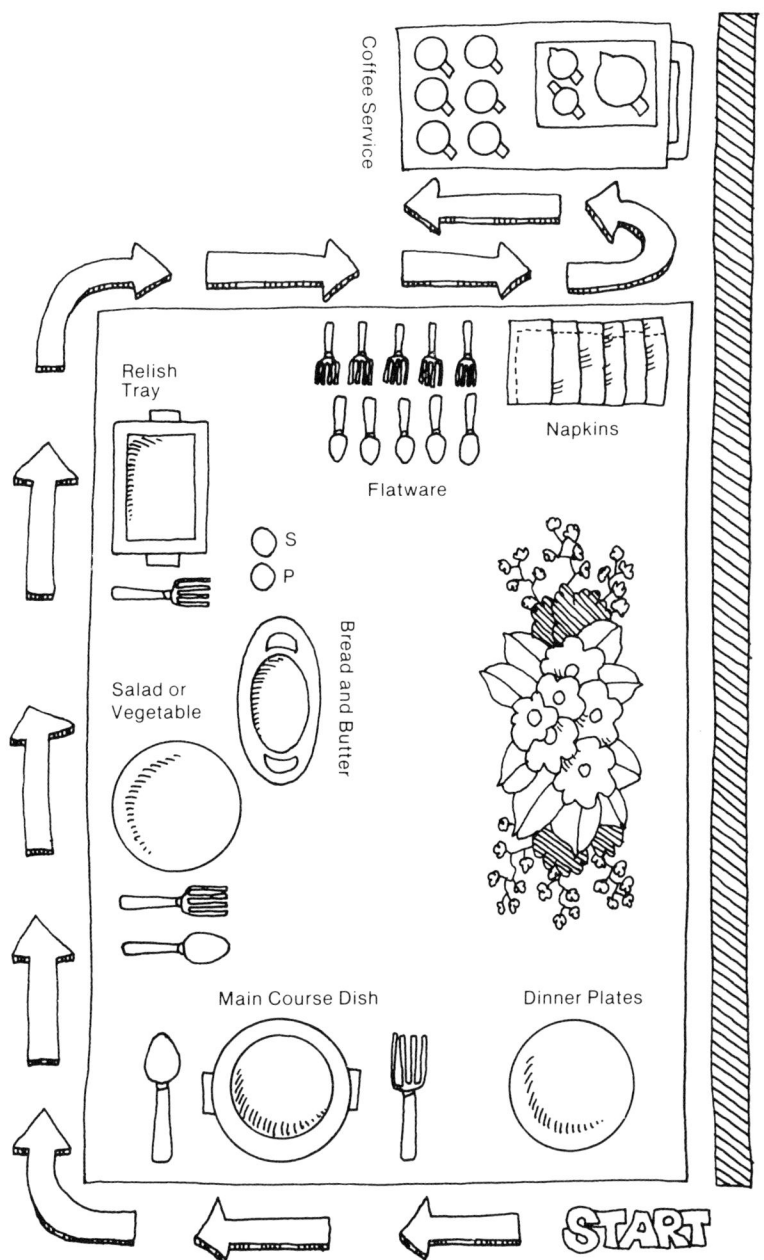

Special Occasion Settings

On holidays and special occasions, when the food and faces are so often familiar, surprise everyone, and treat yourself, by doing something different. Celebrate in an unexpected place. For the anniversary party you are hosting, set a formal table with all its accoutrements — linens, china, crystal, and silver — in the backyard. On the Fourth of July, invite your guests to the beach and serve a picnic. Have a tea party for your daughter's fifth birthday. See in the New Year with a light but succulent supper in bed — and serve it on breakfast trays. Don't be timid. A change in ritual is always enticing.

If you would rather design a traditional table, however, let the surprise come from the kitchen. Much like the poet with countless ways to say, I love you, a clever host knows how to say welcome, in a variety of fashions. One of the most expressive is with the menu. Serve a guest's favorite dish, or roast a goose or suckling pig. Make your own pickles or pâté; flambé bananas for dessert, or bake a mountain of fresh filled, sugar coated cream puffs.

But do keep in mind that holidays and times of special celebrations tend to be frantic; make it easier on yourself by preparing all you can in advance. The idea, after all, is to get out of the kitchen, not to be chained to it. If you wish, forget the surprises. In the end, it is your good spirits that make a holiday gathering or special occasion special for your guests — and for you.

Independence Day

Instead of a cookout, try a takeout. On July Fourth, Labor Day, Memorial Day, or a summer birthday. Plan a menu you can prepare ahead; when the time comes, just pack the hamper, ice the drinks, make the salad, and go. Head for the hills, or the beach. Present it with style. A tabletop is a tabletop, even if it is on the ground, and should be as thoughtfully arranged as one of conventional height.

Thanks to the many colorful and compact new designs in paper and plastics, even the most elaborate picnic can be done with ease. On the opposite page, you can see how well the specially-designed elements work together. Insulated pitchers and jugs to keep beverages hot or cold; plate trays and serving pieces so simple to transport. Individual flatware settings are tucked into terry cloth towels, about the handiest idea ever for picnic napkins. Underneath it all, the latest and most sensible ground mat: a quilted mover's blanket, now made in fashionably bright colors and available in stores.

Remember the little things. Before you leave home, check to be certain you have left nothing important behind. (Once the picnic is under way, you cannot dash into the house for more spoons or ice.) A bottle opener, corkscrew (if you are having wine), napkins, more napkins and then some, and foil-packed towelettes are a few of the extras. A first aid kit too, complete with sunburn ointment, insect repellent, and balms for minor cuts and scratches.

Picnics should be carefree, and guests encouraged to do whatever suits their fancy. Some will opt for strenuous sport, while others are perfectly content to laze. The considerate host will anticipate guests' preferences with a supply of towels, mats, and pillows, and games for youngsters and adults.

And consider what you cannot control—the weather. Should the day be breezy, be prepared with small but weighty objects to ground cloths, clothing and napkins. Heavy napkin rings are a thought; so too are fisherman's lead sinkers, should you have any about.

Anniversary

Anniversaries say sentiment, and together they evoke visions of moonlight out of doors, candlelight and champagne indoors. If the anniversary celebration is a gathering of just a few close friends, a sit-down dinner beautifully presented may be all the party plan need involve. Pay honor with a setting such as the one on the opposite page: Use a cloth with a pattern of delicate bouquets, your best china and glasses, and a centerpiece of candles and small, elegantly-wrapped gifts.

A long marriage can inspire any number of themes for the large family celebration. What is most fitting is indeed a family decision. One thought is a centerpiece of cherished family photographs, or one that incorporates the anniversary's particular symbol, be it paper, wood, gold, or silver. Then, too, you might use a trip the couple once took to set the style. If it was a vacation in Hawaii, for instance, rekindle their memories with a centerpiece of fruit and exotic flowers surrounded by leis for everyone. An evening in Paris, on the other hand, might be recalled with a bistro setting, and French food, of course. For authentic ambience, go all out and add cabaret music.

The food you are serving can also cue your table decorations if the couple's favorites make up the menu. Chinese, Mexican, or Scandinavian cuisine, for example, inspire lively decorative approaches for the total-look design. If the couple you are feting is elderly, however, consider their physical comfort and dietary requirements. Eating rich food on floor pillows may no longer be their notion of fun. If you are unsure, check with a close friend or relative before putting your party plans in motion. Should gifts be part of the celebration, arrange for the couple to be seated comfortably at a table to open them. Trying to unwrap a bulky package on one's lap, and show enthusiasm at the same time, can be a chore.

Remember that anniversary celebrations need not always be dressy. If season and locale permit, a beach or patio party can be a blue-jeans affair—casual, with food and table settings in keeping. Indoors, the scene might be a family room buffet.

A Child's Birthday

Make the table for a child's party a small extension of the playground—full of entertaining things to do, and "equipment" that is up to exuberant handling. Whatever your decorations, though, be sure there is something for each child to take home. Squabbles are inevitable, so a good supply of favors—enough to go around *plus*—is the better part of wisdom.

Keep things simple: one kind of drink—soda, punch, or fruit juice; ice cream with cake *or* cupcakes, but not both.

Another time and trouble saver is paper: paper plates, cups and table covers. The table opposite is covered with kraft paper. Plenty of crayons stand ready in individual clear plastic holders for the kids to do with as they wish—on the kraft paper, of course. The large white numbers scattered over the table are actually cookie cutters. These and the crayons are the party's "loot."

When possible, hold a child's party outdoors. Otherwise, use a basement playroom (if you have one), an enclosed porch, or the garage—if it is not too dirty, and if the clutter can easily be removed. If your living or dining room are your only alternatives, free as much space as you can for the children. And keep smiling.

Supervision is essential, but children's parties generally run more smoothly if there are not too many hovering adults. You and one willing aide are enough unless you have a houseful of toddlers. Should there be a number of adults, however, prepare a table of light snacks for them in another part of the house. They will welcome the chance to relax, knowing someone else is tending their children.

Two hours is a reasonable length of time for a youngster's party. Schedule games for the first hour, then assemble everyone at the table for the second. Unlike their elders, children seldom judge a party by how long it lasts. What counts is how many exciting things there are to do.

In Celebration of Trays

If you must fetch and carry, do it with a marvelous tray. These tables-in-transit are perfect when a sick child is confined to bed, when your weekend guest deserves to be pampered, or, not the least important, when you deserve to be pampered.

There is no gainsaying it, breakfast in bed is one of life's luxuries. You may have to make it yourself and serve it, but who cares when you can climb back in bed with a white wicker tray such as the one on the opposite page. With delicate china and lovely flatware on a quilted mat (it prevents the dishes from rattling), the morning paper, some of the latest magazines, and a single white flower, you are transformed into a lady of leisure.

For a child well enough to eat but not to get up to do it, make staying in bed a bit more palatable with a few toys on a brightly colored plastic tray. The dishes, too, are plastic and colorful, while the flatware has a thick, easy-to-hold handle. Youngsters have an easier time with a footed tray than a flat one, which must be balanced on the lap. Choose a tray with fold-away legs; it is more convenient to store.

The tea tray, opposite, borrows from two worlds and their venerable rituals—the tea ceremony of the Orient, and England's high tea. Adapted for American tastes, the tray and its glazed pottery are functional, muted in color and pure in line.

These three trays are just the beginning. Look for trays in all manner of shapes, sizes, materials, colors—from the humble flat serving tray to the TV table; in silver, brass, Lucite, lacquer, mock tortoise shell, teak, tin; in all the rainbow colors as well as prints, stripes, and plaids.

Consider trays in graduated sizes ranging from the very small to coffee table proportion. Arrange them to form an imposing pyramid for a display of bibelots. Set side by side, staircase-fashion, they are perfect for canapes, drinks, and a vase of flowers. Whatever their size or shape, they are more than simply decorative. They work for you.

Easter Greetings

Tables fresh as crocuses poking through the snow signal a new season's arrival. Bedeck them with bright linens and tableware that echo spring's joyous new mood. Lots of sparkly white, sunny yellows, and sky blues for casual tables, such as the one on the opposite page. And add lilies — they are back in grace as a fashionable flower.

For a dressier production, flatter your basic dinnerware pattern with new accessories. Some of the smartest designs are in clear or frosted glass — chunky and boldly-shaped pieces for holding flowers, candles, even wine and dessert. Some are textured. Still others have the delicate haze and flowing shape of Lalique. Because they are colorless, they always harmonize with their surroundings.

The air is full of new ideas in tableware. What better time than spring to give some of them a whirl. Double and triple layer linens, as well as plates. Add splashes of color — individual covered soup bowls in bright lacquer, or salad plates with a rim-to-rim pattern of flowers bigger than nature ever intended.

Flatware manufacturers have not been idle. Today there are multitudes of new designs in intriguing shapes. So if the family sterling languishes in the bank vault, has been sold, or never existed in the first place, now is the time to give stainless steel its due and try the avant-garde — wide handles stripped of embellishment, or thick with pattern and detailing. And blades, tines, and spoon bowls heavily under the influence of science fiction, but functional nevertheless, and very fit for use on earth.

If spring is here, can summer be far behind? And with it one-dish meals to cut down on time spent in the kitchen. Splurge on an oven-to-table piece in beautifully decorated fine porcelain, or be casual with an oven-proof casserole in handsome porcelain-clad iron.

Should you go overboard on something and cause friends to look at you askance — say it's spring fever.

Winter's Festive Board

'Tis the season to think hearty. Golden brown roasts and fowl on large platters. Tureens of rich stews. Bowls heaped with steaming vegetables. This is the time of year when menus are most apt to influence table settings, mainly because large serving pieces need space. The amenities—centerpieces and candles—must make room for them. Consider the arrangement of your table from two points of view: for convenience in serving and eating, and for appearance. Will the table *look* too crowded; will guests *be* crowded? The comfort of your guests, after all, is your primary concern, so have a number of alternatives if space is a problem.

The simplest solution is the buffet, as seen on the opposite page, with all dishes from main courses to dessert set on a side table. (If you are lucky enough to own a tureen masquerading as a duck complete with a goose-neck ladle, use it.) Guests can help themselves, then sit at the family table laid with silver, napkins, and condiments.

If there are too many people for even this flexible arrangement, use tray tables or card tables in an adjoining room. Dress them up with colorful linens and vases of flowers or greens. Floor-length cloths look especially pretty on card tables, but avoid them on tray tables—they get in the way of one's feet and knees.

When children are present, fix a table just for them. Make it attractive and colorful, and perhaps include a game or soft toy they can amuse themselves with during the meal. Felt hand puppets are delightful surprises, and unbreakable. Keep in mind that children are part of the festivities. They and their table belong in the midst of the gathering, not isolated from it.

Bring warm colors to winter tables—combine tangy oranges and red to make a cozy backdrop for china that is predominantly white. Deep rich plum tones, burgundy hues, and dark browns are appealing with floral patterned china as well as more casual stoneware.

New Year's Eve Dinner

A poll of your friends might reveal they prefer a quiet celebration to the traditionally riotous one. If so, plan a late supper with light but elegant food. And fashion an atmosphere that is a bit on the lavish side—everyone's psyche can do with coddling on this evening.

Have lots of candlelight and be generous with accents and the centerpiece. Use your prettiest china and linens. A floor-length cloth adds drama. So does gleaming silver. Or delicate place mats on a bare table of polished wood. The choice is yours; take the loveliest route.

If your guest list is small, serve supper in the dining room. If it is large, return once again to the buffet and seat guests at small tables in the living room. For you who live in warm climates, a New Year's Eve supper under the midnight sky would be beautiful.

Allow yourself ample time to arrange your room and decorate the table or tables. It almost goes without saying, but do try to have dishes you can prepare in advance. Order plenty of ice and store it in insulated containers close to the bar, at which guests serve themselves. As with any party, you will want to spend as much time with your guests as possible and not be bothered with myriad last-minute details.

How to bid farewell to the old year and hail the new? If noisemakers, a blaring radio, funny hats, and streamers are not the touch you had in mind, why not make midnight a time to give? At each place setting, put a small and beautifully wrapped gift to be opened on the stroke of twelve.

On the opposite page, an enchanting setting to share with old friends and usher in a new year. Its theme is familiar; put yourself into the picture and vary it as you wish. Dare to be different. That, after all, is what the art of table decoration is all about.

Acknowledgements

We are grateful to the following manufacturers for the use of their fine products in the preceding pages:

Aynsley Bone China, 8, 47, 82

Belleek Perian China, 86

Bluegate Candle Co. (Pentland Gift Sources, Inc.), 27, 53, 58, 62

Colonial Candle Co. of Cape Cod, Inc., division of General Housewares Corp. Giftware Group, 8, 14, 42, 65, 90

Arthur Court Designs, Inc., candlesticks, 65; tureen and ladle, 90

Denby Ltd., Inc., dinnerware; crystal, 20, 22; flatware, 22; gift, 37

Doulton and Co., Inc., 61

Dulken & Derrick Inc., silk flowers, 34, 49

Alfred G. Fein Sales Corp., tray, 86

Fitz and Floyd, candle holders, 14; dinnerware, 28, 29, 50

The Gorham Co., china, crystal, sterling, 21

Hammacher Schlemmer, glassware, 50; rugs, 58; cookie cutters, 85; tray, 86

Ingrid Ltd., dinnerware and stainless, 81, 86

Jacques Jugeat, Inc., 65

H. E. Lauffer Co., Inc., dinnerware, 62; crystal, 34, 44, 62, 81, 82, 89; stainless, 62, 66

Leacock Co., Inc., linens (Pentland Gift Sources, Inc.), 53

Lenox China, 23, 58, 90; Lenox Crystal, 23, 58, 65, 90

Lion Ribbon Co., Inc., 61, 78

Lunt Silversmiths, sterling, 8, 61; candlesticks, 54; stainless, 29, 86

Martex Towels, 81, 86

Mikasa, dinnerware, 53, 57, 86, 89; accessories, 57, 66; crystal, 57, 66

Naif (Villeroy & Boch), dinnerware, 68

Ocean House Linens (Pentland Gift Sources, Inc.), 86

Oneida Silversmiths, stainless, 86

Oxford Hall Silversmiths, stainless 53, 58, 85

Reed & Barton Silversmiths, sterling, 23, 28, 47, 54; silverplate, 20, 33, 41, 47, 49, 82; stainless, 65, 90

Stanley Roberts Inc., stainless, 88

Romatch by Ross-Mathai Corp., linens, 8, 21, 22, 47, 50, 62, 65, 66, 82, 86, 90

Textol Linens, division of General Housewares Corp. Giftware Group, 20, 29, 49, 86

Waterford Glass, Inc., 8, 44, 47, 82, 86

The Wedgwood Group, dinnerware, 49, 54; crystal, 54

F. W. Woolworth Co., dinnerware, 27

Index

anniversaries, 83
ashtrays and cigarette holders, 24, 70

birthday, child's, 84
breakfast settings, 72
   tray, 87
buffet
   circular, 74
   French Provincial, 64
   New Year's Eve, 92
   Scandinavian, 63
   three-sided, 76
   winter feasts, 91

candles, 17, 23
   centerpieces, 43
   colored, 13, 17, 43
   fitting into holder, 17
   height, 17
   white, 13
candle holders, 15, 17
centerpieces
   breakfast setting, 72
   buffet, 74
   candles, 43
   for children, 36
   flowers, fresh, 32-33
   flowers, silk and dried, 34-35
   fruits and vegetables, fresh, 40-41
   fun, 36-37
   high, 16
   holders for, 16
   luncheon setting, 72
   plants, live, 16, 38-39
   selecting, 31
   settings (themes) and, 44-67 *passim*
children
   centerpieces for, 36
   party, 84
   table for, 91
   tray for, 87
coffee sets, 15
Colonial setting, 54-55
color schemes, 13, 19, 45, 46
Country Kitchen setting, 52-53

dinnerware
   breakfast, 72-73
   buffets, 74-77
   choosing, 10
   Easter setting, 88-89
   floral English traditional, 46-47
   luncheon, 72-73
   mixing and matching, 26-27
   place settings, formal and informal, 69-72
   settings (themes) and, 44-67 *passim*
   tray service, 86-87

Early American setting, 48-49
Easter, 88-89

flatware
   breakfast setting, 72-73
   buffets, 74-77
   choosing, 12
   luncheon setting, 72-73
   place settings, formal and informal, 69-71
   settings (themes) and, 44-67 *passim*
   tray service, 86-87
floral settings, traditional English, 46-47
flower pots, dressing up, 38-39
flowers
   beaded, 35
   containers, for, 13, 16, 32
   dried, 34-35
   fresh, 23, 32-33, 72
   plastic, 35
   porcelain, 35
   silk, 23, 34-35
food presentation (*see also* Menus)
   buffet, 63, 74, 76
   Oriental, 56-57
formal settings, 69-70
Forties setting, 50-51
French Provincial setting, 64-65
fruit centerpieces, 40-41

glassware and stemware
   breakfast setting, 72
   choosing, 11
   luncheon setting, 72
   place settings, formal and informal, 69-71
   settings (themes) and, 44-67 *passim*

informal settings, 69-71

linens, 13, 15,
   breakfast setting, 72-73
   buffets, 74-77
   Easter setting, 88-89
   luncheon setting, 72-73
   New Year's Eve setting, 92-93
   settings (themes) and, 44-67
   tray service, 86-87
   winter tables, 90-91
luncheon settings, 72-73

menus (*see also* Food presentation)
   anniversary, 83
   child's party, 84
   luncheon, 72
   Oriental, 56
   Scandinavian, 63
   setting theme, 45
menu stands, 70
mixing and matching, 26-27

napkin ring, 24-25, 70, 80
napkins, 13, 15
New Year's Eve, 92-93

Oceans and Islands settings, 58-59
Oriental setting, 56-57
ovenware, 15

picnics, 80-81
place card holder, 24, 70
place mats, 13, 15
plants, live, 16, 38-39
   pots, dressing up, 38-39

Scandinavian setting, 62-63
seating, 69, 92
serving dishes, 15, 24
   coffee and tea sets, 15
settings, 44
   Anniversary, 82-83
   breakfast, 72-73
   buffets, 74-77
   child's party, 84-85
   Colonial, 54-55
   Country Kitchen, 52-53
   Early American, 48-49
   Easter, 88-89
   formal, 70-71
   French Provincial, 64-65
   Funky Forties, 50-51
   Independence Day, 80-81
   informal, 70-71
   luncheon, 72-73
   New Year's Eve dinner, 92-93
   nostalgia, 51
   occasions, special, 78-93
   Oceans and Islands, 58-59
   Oriental, 56-57
   picnics, 80-81
   Scandinavian, 62-63
   Stripped down modern, 66-67
   Traditional English floral, 46-47
   tray, 86-87
   types of, 69-77
   Victorian, 60-61
   Winter, 90-91
silverware
   flatware (*see also* Flatware), 12
   serving pieces, 15
stemware, *see* Glassware

table elements (*see also* specific
   subjects), 9-17
   coordinating, 18-67
   dinnerware, 10
   flatware, 12
   glassware and stemware, 11
   miscellaneous, 13-17
   mixing and matching, 26-29
   settings (themes) and, 44-67
   types of table settings and, 68-77
themes for settings, 46-67
tea sets, 15
tea tray, 87
trays, 13, 24, 86-87

vases, 16
vegetable centerpieces, 40-41
Victorian setting, 60

wine servers, 13
winter tables, 90-91